ALL ABOUT BREEDING
BUDGERIGARS

Mervin F. Roberts

Photographs by Louise Van der Meid (except as credited otherwise). Thanks are due to James Brown, Darrol Grant, Barbara Patterson, Shirley Prather, and Betty Travis for allowing their birds and their facilities to be photographed.

Title-page photo by Harry V. Lacey.

Distributed in the UNITED STATES by T.F.H. Publications, Inc., 211 West Sylvania Avenue, Neptune City, NJ 07753; in CANADA by H & L Pet Supplies Inc., 27 Kingston Crescent, Kitchener, Ontario N2B 2T6; Rolf C. Hagen Ltd., 3225 Sartelon Street, Montreal 382 Quebec; in ENGLAND by T.F.H. Publications Limited, 4 Kier Park, Ascot, Berkshire SL5 7DS; in AUSTRALIA AND THE SOUTH PACIFIC by T.F.H. (Australia) Pty. Ltd., Box 149, Brookvale 2100 N.S.W., Australia; in NEW ZEALAND by Ross Haines & Son, Ltd., 18 Monmouth Street, Grey Lynn, Auckland 2 New Zealand; in SINGAPORE AND MALAYSIA by MPH Distributors (S) Pte., Ltd., 601 Sims Drive, # 03/07/21, Singapore 1438; in the PHILIPPINES by Bio-Research, 5 Lippay Street, San Lorenzo Village, Makati Rizal; in SOUTH AFRICA by Multipet Pty. Ltd., 30 Turners Avenue, Durban 4001. Published by T.F.H. Publications Inc., Ltd. the British Crown Colony of Hong Kong.

Contents

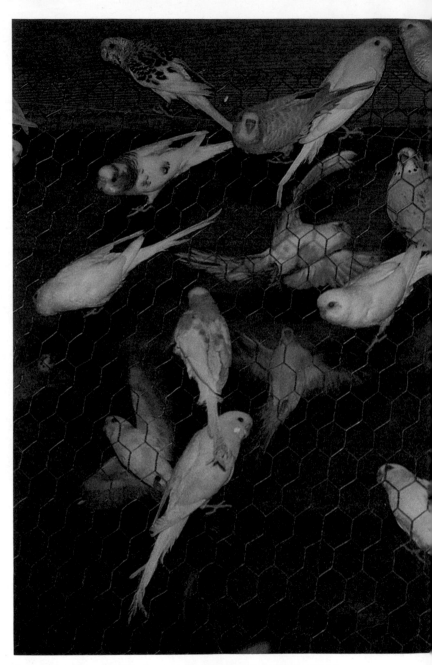

Several color varieties housed together in a roomy flight.

Of all the birds that are kept as pets, budgerigars are the most popular. Photo: Harry V. Lacey.

Preface

There is no shortage of literature about budgies, and much of what exists is excellent. However, this book was written for special readers, people who have tried and failed to breed budgies and people who haven't started because it seemed too difficult or too expensive.

Well, I cannot promise you a rose garden, but I did write what I thought was a good book about these delightful little parrots in 1956, and I have been involved with various aspects of ornithology for nearly fifty years, so perhaps I can help you to help your birds without leading you to tears or bankruptcy. Before you read further, please don't jump to the conclusion that the task is as easy as falling off a log or as profitable as investing your money in a blue-chip security. Breeding budgies is not easy, and no one I know about ever got really rich at it; but breeding budgerigars can be an interesting challenge, and many people of all ages all over the world find it to be great fun. Those who are good at it break even, with luck.

This book is provided with a Table of Contents and an Index. The sections are fairly short and are carefully titled so that you can jump around easily. It need not be read like a detective novel starting on page one.

After you have mastered those things which you must do to encourage your birds to breed successfully, it will be time enough to learn about color genetics, show standards, training, and exhibiting your birds. For these subjects, I suggest you look at the books mentioned at the end of this one, for certainly there is a great deal more that can be said. But for here and now, let's get started by simply breeding budgies, simply.

Not all budgies are used in breeding programs; some are sold as pets instead. A singly-kept budgie can be easily hand-tamed and will amuse itself with spray millet (*above*), wooden ladders (*below*), and toys (*facing page*).

The Name of the Bird

The current scientific name of the *Budgerigar* is *Melopsittacus undulatus*. It has also been known by several common English names since it was first described in 1794. Those older common names have been dropped because they were wrong for one reason or another. When I wrote about these birds in 1956 they were commonly called "parakeets" here in the U.S.A. This is a bad name because there happen to be other, unrelated parrots which are also called parakeets. "Lovebird" is another name which was applied to *M. undulatus,* but more usually to a group of small African parrots with short tails. These African species were known as lovebirds long before budgies came into the marketplace as caged pets. So "lovebird" is out, and "parakeet" is out, and "budgerigar" is in—with good reason. This name comes from the Australian Aborigines—it means "good bird" and possibly suggests that it is a good bird to eat. As recently as 1970, books by British authors would sometimes call our bird the "shell parrakeet" (notice the double *r*); this is still another name which seems to have lost favor.

What Budgies Do Naturally

These little Australian parrots live in flocks and communicate noisily. Flocks permit warnings of danger and better opportunities for escape. Flocks also expedite foraging, since a successful bird signals the others that food is nearby.

Budgies eat millet, canary seed, oat groats, and other small seeds. When you are getting started, begin with a budgie mix from your pet shop. Later, if you keep a number of birds, buy bird seed in bulk and make up your own mixture. Most budgies go through life eating nothing but grain and leafy vegetables, but some will enjoy grapes and other fruit. They will gnaw on a cuttlebone or a ham bone; they will enjoy diced, hard-boiled (20-minute) chicken eggs, shell included. Some will eat mealworms and some will not. Of course they drink water; and it should be fresh, and it should be provided from a clean container.

Budgies may bathe—then again, they may not. They will sit in the rain, roll in wet leaves or wet grass, and certainly act like they enjoy these activities, but some are inconsistent about bathing in a dish. If your birds don't wash themselves today, okay—but you cannot make up their minds for them. They may just bathe tomorrow, especially if it is a dry, sunny, warm day and the water is shallow, at room temperature, and clean. If they see other birds bathing, they may be inclined to try also.

Budgies whistle and chatter at each other, preen each other, argue with each other, sometimes fight, but rarely injure or kill each other.

Budgies are awake most of the daylight hours, but they may snooze awhile on a hot summer afternoon. Budgies don't fly at night, but they don't necessarily sleep all night either. Nestlings might squeak a bit, and the hen might just feed them.

Budgies molt from time to time, but they never become naked or flightless. A hen might pluck a few feathers from her breast to enlarge the bare skin area necessary for the transfer of heat to incubate her eggs.

Nests are in cavities, but no nest materials are carried in. The few feathers in the nest box were molted, or plucked there. Eggs are laid on punky wood in tree hollows, or on bare wood or wood chips or on vermiculite which bird keepers sometimes put in a nest box. Nest boxes should be provided with bottom boards which have concave depressions in order to keep as many as eight or even ten of these white eggs together.

Eggs hatch in the order in which they were laid, and the first young to hatch tend to keep the unhatched eggs warm. Hens alone incubate the eggs and feed the newborn chicks. Cocks feed the hens and the older chicks.

Under ideal conditions, budgies will breed constantly and could eventually die of exhaustion. Here is a place where you can help with some thoughtful management.

When you watch your birds carefully, you will notice that they are busy most of their waking hours. Watch a pair and perhaps you will see some or all of the following things. These activities are all "normal."

The male will be most attentive and prone to copulate

Budgerigars are playful little birds whose activities include feeding (*above*), bathing (*below*), and swinging on swings (*facing page*).

with the female in the early morning, after sunrise but before 8 A.M. He will feed his mate, tenderly, attentively.

The female will duck into the nest box frequently before she begins to lay. There might be a week or so between the first mating and the first egg. It might take that long for the egg to mature after it was fertilized. If you pile a little hill of sawdust in the concave you will soon discover whether the hen has been practicing for her next big project.

The female will chew at the nest box or perhaps at a piece of softwood which you might provide. Many nest boxes have been demolished over the years by hen budgies.

Just a few days prior to laying, the droppings of the hen will be larger than they had been.

Sometimes budgies throw out all the punky wood and sawdust that you so thoughtfully placed in the concave. It would have been a good cushion for the eggs. Should you replace it? I don't know.

The hen may sit on her first egg, but just sitting and actually incubating are not the same. Birds have bare skin areas which transmit their body warmth to their eggs. Feathers are great insulators; if a hen sits with her feathers tight to her body, no heat will reach the egg and incubation will not commence.

It will be normal for you to wonder if the eggs are fertile and if incubation is proceeding. You can "candle" eggs with a bright light after a few days of incubation, and you may see red streaks developing on the surface of the egg yolk. This is the embryo developing. The more frequently you handle the eggs, the greater the risk of killing the very thing you wish to propagate. Restrain yourself; let Mother Nature do her thing.

After about eighteen days of incubation, each egg will hatch. The chick will cut its way out by using a tiny, thornlike pin on its beak. Soon after hatching, this tool is gone and forgotten. Let the bird get out of its shell unaided. Novices kill many chicks because they get impatient and think they can help. The very few chicks that die as they hatch were probably malformed or too weak to survive anyway.

The Timetable of Budgie Life

• A pair mates. Copulation might take place once daily until incubation commences. The hen will lay her first egg about seven to ten days after that first mating. Usually one egg will be laid every other day. About five eggs make an average clutch, but sometimes as many as ten fertile eggs are laid by the same hen in the same nest.

• The hen begins to incubate her eggs after she has laid one or two.

• The cock feeds the hen while she alone incubates her clutch.

• Each egg hatches after eighteen days of incubation.

• Both parents feed the youngsters, and the cock continues to feed the hen as well, until the youngest chick is no longer being brooded.

• The chicks' eyes open when they are about seven days old.

• They leave the nest about four weeks after hatching, but the parents continue to feed them until about their sixth week.

• A youngster, or bar-head, molts for the first time when it is about three months old, but budgies are not considered to be adult until they are about twelve months old.

• An average budgie lives about ten years, and some have been known to live to age twenty. Budgies are most useful as breeders between their second and seventh years.

Cages and Aviaries

An aviary is a walk-in structure in which many birds are kept. A cage is a portable enclosure for no more than a few birds.

If you want to be sure, absolutely sure, which cock sired a clutch of eggs, you must segregate your birds by pairs. If a hen is receptive and her mate is not alert, really alert, another cock might just be at the right place at the right time.

If you want to get started simply and economically, you must give up any ideas you may have had about controlled breeding, line-breeding, genetics, application of

Courtship behavior often includes allopreening, that is, grooming each other's feathers (*above*). Soon after a pair copulate, the hen will lay her eggs (*below*), and these will be incubated for about eighteen days. The youngsters are reared in their nest for approximately four weeks (*facing page*).

Mendelian laws, and so on. It is so much easier to put three mature males and three mature females into one large enclosure with five or six nest boxes and one watering dish (plus a spare) and one feeder (plus a spare). To house three pairs separately, consider the extra effort involved for furnishing feed and water, cleaning, opening and closing doors, and so on. Also consider the cost of those cages.

Consider too the flying space these birds can enjoy if they are grouped. A pair might be caged in five cubic feet, where the long dimension of the cage is three feet. The exercise of flight is so valuable to breeding birds and so easy to achieve that you should seriously favor the single large enclosure and one small colony rather than several smaller enclosures. What you will lose is the certainty of parentage. Remember, I offer you a simple approach to breeding budgies. You lose some control with a small colony, but you save a lot of effort and some money.

Unless you are a really good tin knocker and/or cabinet maker, I suggest that if you opt for breeding cages, you should buy them. Some cages are obtainable knocked down; this makes shipping easier. But, no matter, don't reinvent the wheel, and don't design still another bird cage.

It doesn't matter whether a well-made cage is plywood or particle board or all metal. What does matter is that it should be easy to clean and easy to get into. Nest boxes are often mounted outside cages, but inside aviaries. This sometimes becomes a problem for "difficult" caged pairs. They may want to crawl over the nest box before going into it.

Ideally, the metal should all be stainless steel, but speaking practically, this is very expensive. Chrome-plated or galvanized steel is considered by most people to be perfectly adequate. You may see advertisements for knocked-down walk-in cages—you might call them prefabricated aviaries. These are great for breeding budgies. Just be sure, if you order one through an advertisement, that the mesh is metal and is fine enough to keep mice out. I prefer three-eighth-inch mesh, but you may have to settle for one-half-inch openings. Avoid wood lattice or wood screen. This might be okay for finches, but a budgie can easily chew through even flame-hardened bamboo. The only wood products you should place inside a budgie breeding cage are nest boxes and perches. Some experienced aviculturists favor perches of oval or square cross-section because a slippery perch makes copulation difficult. Infertile eggs might result if the perch is not secure or is difficult to grab. A sandpaper sleeve on a perch is a mistake; don't use it.

Well-made housing for budgies will cost a good deal of money whether you choose cages or an aviary. You should not skimp on quality. If your cash supply is limited, you should start small rather than shoddy. Ideally, here are some things you should be thinking about.

Avoid the kinds of cages usually available for pet birds. Most of them don't offer nest-box room or accessibility. They are hard to get into if you wish to catch a bird, and they don't lend themselves to stacking. They are designed to look good themselves and to make the bird look good on display in your home. This is not necessarily the best place to breed budgies.

Provide for a back-up door to prevent escapes. If you have a walk-in aviary, it should surely include this feature. One door should be so low that you must duck to get in. Many escapes take place over your head, as you enter.

In parts of the country where there are mosquitoes and flies (almost everywhere), you should be using insect screening in addition to what is necessary to keep your birds from escaping.

An outdoor aviary might be made of structural members an inch-and-a-half or so thick, with insect screening on the outside and a coarse, heavier screen on the inside. This should reduce the possibility of disease transmitted by wild birds.

You should read at least one of the books mentioned later in this one before you build or buy anything more than you already have.

If possible, arrange the enclosure so that you can view your birds with the light coming over your shoulder

Nest boxes (*above*) can be either purchased or made at home, depending on your time, finances, and the resources available. The same is true for breeding cages and feed hoppers (*facing page*), which in this case are metal.

rather than into your eyes. Your birds will look better, and you will be able to spot problems more readily.

Assume that every rat, opossum, cat, dog, fox, raccoon, and weasel is your sworn enemy—just waiting for a door ajar or a bit of rusty, weakened screening. Mice are not predators, but they are pests. They soil and steal food; also they will keep your birds awake at night.

Be reconciled to the fact that an escaped bird is a lost bird. Spend your effort and money on precautions and not on high-speed chases with nets and ladders.

Dry Goods

Besides live budgies, the pet dealer offers many products useful in keeping budgies, from seed mix to treats to toys to nest boxes. Some of these fall into the categories of necessities, but others are suited to particular purposes. A ferris wheel or a cart or a seed bell is fine for a single caged pet that needs exercise and entertainment, but these are not the sorts of things that will induce a hen to lay or a cock to feed the fledglings. My suggestion to a novice budgie *breeder* is to keep the cage or aviary as open as possible. Arrange perches and nest boxes and landing places and feeding stations near the walls, and leave the central area clear for flight. Most budgies I've seen would rather fly than swing or climb or ring bells or admire themselves in mirrors.

Feeding and watering devices should be heavy enough so that they cannot tip over. They should be light-colored or clear glass so you can easily determine if they are even the least bit dirty. They should be resistant to heat so you can sterilize them with boiling water. They should be large enough to carry the birds through a weekend if you plan to go away. Unless you have a well-trained, reliable person to fill in for you, the risks of omission for a weekend are probably less than the risks of commission. A novice could easily do tremendous harm by leaving a door unlatched or letting the cat slip in. Experienced breeders have found that duplicate feeding and watering arrangements in a room sealed off from intruders will carry a cage or aviary of birds over a few days quite nicely. If you think your mated pairs will miss you, you had better go back to keeping one bird as a house pet and give up all thoughts of breeding budgies. So, keep your furnishings simple, strong, easy to clean, and adequate to provide the necessities for two or three days; leave the toys and gadgets for the single pet cage-bird.

Choosing and Pairing Budgies

If we look at wild budgies in Australia, we will find no runts, no french molters, no wry-necks, no drooping wings, no deformed bills. Mother Nature takes care of that; sweet, kind, gentle, and compassionate she isn't. She is ruthless. Now the ball is in your court; you can produce any grade of bird you desire. I suggest you throw out sympathy and promptly forget any "pet" names these birds may have been given. Give people names, but give birds numbers. Treat them with thoughtful, gentle care. But if you want to breed birds, you should erase any sentimentality.

Buy the best birds you can afford. Avoid the fancy colors—albinos, lutinos, even pied. Settle for common, dark, solid colors such as green or blue. Choose big, robust, broad-chested, large-headed, straight-tailed, active birds. Try to get either proven breeding pairs or young adults. For starters, I suggest you skip any bargain birds—ask yourself, "Why are they so cheap?" Ask yourself why these off-quality birds are not in breeders' aviaries and breeders' cages. Why are they available for sale? Often it is because they will make good pets, but the breeders found that they were no good in the nest box. As a beginner, you don't need that. Find a dealer who has or can get you genuine, active breeders. Be prepared to pay a fair price, probably as much as two or three times the price of ordinary budgies intended for sale as singly caged pets.

How do we pick pairs? Begin by getting equal numbers of each sex. Try to get birds of approximately the same age—ideally a year or two old. Colors don't matter so long as you don't go for the rare and expensive varieties while you are learning. Look for birds in breeding condition. A male's cere should be cobalt blue, and a female's a mahogany brown. Budgies which are out of condition don't display well-colored ceres. Look

Official closed leg bands (*above*) document the year in which a bird was hatched. In those budgerigar varieties in which barring on the head occurs, it indicates a juvenile bird, while the absence of barring signifies adulthood (*below*). In mature budgies, sex can be determined by cere color: in males of most varieties the cere is a bright blue, while in females it is always tan or brown (*facing page*).

for bright blue on males, rich brown on females. "Pairs" is meaningless, as male budgies are notoriously promiscuous. That last sentence was a profound statement. I hope you didn't skim past it.

How do you know how old they are? Simple, but again more costly. Buy only birds with dated, closed bands. The better breeders of the better birds fit every squeaker with a permanent, closed, dated band. You should too.

When you choose your first few pairs, you might want to work with crested birds. Don't do it. Crests will be all right later, but they're not for beginners. Although they seem to be fertile and as able to raise their young as non-crested birds, there is some suspicion of a linkage between the crested gene and a lethal gene, so avoid them in the beginning.

But what is this "few pairs"? you ask. Well, that's how it is. Two budgies of opposite sex may be a pair, but if you want to breed this species there should be, ideally, at least three pairs within sight and hearing of each other. Three pairs in three separate, closely situated cages, or in one large aviary or flight cage with at least one additional nest box. This is what you need if you want good results, promptly. Adult budgies stimulate each other to nest and breed. A pair of canaries are self-starters, and so are chickens and pigeons. When we get to budgies, one pair is not always a breeding pair right away, but two or three pairs near each other frequently become active breeders promptly. This is something many people don't know, but every experienced breeder knows and capitalizes on this fact of nature.

Everyone who is the least bit romantic knows what a pair is, but with budgies, I suggest you would do well to read on. The first egg will be laid between the seventh and tenth day after the first mating. Since this mating could have happened at 7 A.M. or some other early hour, it is unlikely that you witnessed it; but no matter, they really didn't need you then or there. It is possible that the one mating will provide sufficient sperm to fertilize all the eggs in the clutch. It is also possible that subsequent matings might be necessary to ensure that all the eggs develop. It is possible too that, after the first mating, the hen in a colony situation might accept courtship from still another cock. This is why it is advisable, in a beginner's colony-breeding establishment, to keep only one homozygous color or bird. Then, even if you are not certain of the parentage, at least you haven't mongrelized the color.

A few years hence you will be able to improve some colors by crossbreeding, but here and now I suggest you stick to simple basics until you master them.

Sexing Budgies

Young budgies, the experts will warn you, are not always easy to sex correctly, and older birds will sometimes confuse even the experts. So, what should you do? One reasonable option is to buy proven pairs. This will be more expensive than if you purchase individuals, but you will have solved the problem.

Another reasonable option, if you have the space available, is to buy a number of youngsters chosen randomly but selected carefully for quality. You might be able to get three or four first-class juveniles of unknown or undetermined sex for the same money necessary to buy one proven pair. I suggest that you start out with all your birds of the same color. Breeders of quality stock spend years refining color and pattern; if you have something good, don't mongrelize it before you know what you are doing.

Should you elect this latter option and go for a group of juveniles, how many do you need to buy? Good question! The answer is tied to some simple biology and some fascinating mathematics—which someone else has already worked out for us. Mother Nature ordains that 50% will become females. I know of a few bright, 16-year-old high-school biology students who will remind me that parthenogenetically produced lizards and rabbits and turkeys are always the same sex; but we are concerned here only with *fertilized* birds' eggs.

The 50-50 ratio is true enough only if there is a sufficiently large random sample. Let me reduce this to an absurdity in order to make the point. If a hen has a clutch of only one egg, we will have to agree that there is a 50-50 chance that it will be, say, a male. If she lays only

A hen budgie sits close to her nestlings to provide warmth and security (*above*). Normally the hen's cere is tan or light brown (*below*); however, as the cere darkens, as it has on the female on the facing page, it is apparent that she has come into breeding condition.

two eggs, either egg could be either sex. There could be one of each sex, or two females, or two males. Each egg still has a 50-50 chance of being a male. With two eggs, the possibilities are apparent even without writing them down. Yes, we surely must agree the odds are 25% that there will be two males, 25% that there will be two females, and 50% that there will be one of each sex. Anyone who is involved in animal husbandry and any patriarch, king, or potentate who hopes to perpetuate a line of descent through an unbroken series of sons will come up against these odds. They are inescapable. If you don't like to gamble, you can call them probabilities.

More than three hundred years ago, the French genius Blaise Pascal worked out a table of probabilities for us, and it is as true today as it was then. Briefly, he tells us what the chances are for any sample consisting of two equally possible outcomes, like sex. Let's apply it to the number of chicks in a budgie nest box. Start with a clutch of one egg in the first column and read across.

Size of clutch	Odds all will be the same sex	Odds there will be at least one of the opposite sex
1	1 in 2	—
2	1 in 4	1 in 2, or 50%
3	1 in 8	3 in 4, or 75%
4	1 in 16	7 in 8, or 87.5%
5	1 in 32	15 in 16, or 93.8%
6	1 in 64	31 in 32, or 96.9%
7	1 in 128	63 in 64, or 98.4%
8	1 in 256	127 in 128, or 99.2%

This means that if there are two eggs (as above), there will be a 1-in-4, or 25%, chance that both will be female. There will also be a 25% chance that both will be male. There will also be a 1-in-2, or 50%, chance that there will be one of each.

Consider for a moment a clutch of six eggs. Pascal tells us that there is only one chance in 64 (1/64) that all six will be male. There is also one chance in 64 (1/64) that all six will be female. This accounts for 2/64 of the possible arrangements of the sexes in a clutch of six fertile eggs. So now we have one chance in thirty-two that all will be the same sex. The remaining thirty-one out of thirty-two chances (96.9%) are that there will be *at least one* of the opposite sex in a random sample of six. As a matter of fact, there is even a good chance of two pairs in six eggs.

Pascal gives us this and still more information in the form of a triangle bearing his name which appears in many textbooks. Here is where that bright 16-year-old high-school student can be useful. Get a copy of Pascal's Triangle; it will even give you the odds for the second and third pairs in that random sample of six chicks.

One neat extension of the table you have been working with is that if you start with six birds and are able to pull out a pair, you can then go back into the table for four remaining randomly chosen birds and see what the odds are that you can come up with a second pair. Obviously they are not as good. With four birds, there is an 87.5% chance that one of the opposite sex will be present.

The larger the number you have to work with, the better the chances of ending up with both sexes represented. That was obvious from the start; the chart simply gives us the odds.

The reason for our concern, as I mentioned earlier, is that it is not easy for a beginner to determine the sex of a young budgie. If you want to keep some of your production for future breeding stock, you must become proficient at sexing juveniles or you must remain patient and keep a good number of chicks until their secondary sex characteristics become apparent.

Some of these clues to sex are mentioned elsewhere, but for the sake of convenience I will list as many as I can think of here to help you guess the sex of your birds. Once you are reasonably sure, you should place a colored plastic band on the bird so you can easily spot it again when you need to know. These bands are available in many colors; you might, for example, choose pink and blue. Remember that until a female lays an egg, your best effort is still just a guess.

Males: more prone to talk or mimic people; are sometimes larger headed; are narrower between the pelvic bones; are shiny bright blue in the cere when in

All of the flight feathers have grown in on this juvenile (*above*); the tight plumage gives it a smooth, sleek appearance. Youngsters (*facing page*), once fully fledged and self-sufficient, are usually separated from their parents and placed in a flight of their own.

breeding condition; try to feed females when they are courting; have an intense pinkness of the cere as fledglings; are polygamous when mating but monogamous with parental care.

Females: are more inclined to search for nest sites; are wider than males between pelvic bones; have chocolate brown, wrinkled ceres when in breeding condition; are inclined to bite harder; have white or mother-of-pearl colored ceres as fledglings; are sometimes careless or promiscuous when ardent males are present; are belligerent toward the nests and progeny of other females.

A large chapter or even a small book could be written about the color of the cere of a budgie. Its color and texture are a clue to its sex, its age, its health, and its readiness to breed. The cere is really not very large. Its color is influenced by the feather color of the bird, and the same color can mean different things at different times. For example, many of the "rules" are applicable only to the darker colors in the blue and green series. Albinos, yellows, and the dilute colors are much more difficult to sex. Health also has a profound effect on cere color. This is why I recommend that you start your budgie-breeding experience with a normal dark green strain of healthy birds. Try to get some that are homozygous (pure, or double-factor) and sexing will be much more a sure thing. You still will not be positive, but your batting average will improve. Why do I still "weasel-word"? Well, for one thing, a really old male, too old to fertilize a hen, might develop a wrinkled brown cere; quite a few do if they live long enough.

After considering the old cock, it is appropriate to mention some other clues to the age of a bird. Obviously, before the first molt a normally colored bird will be a bar-head. Also, during the first several months in the life of a budgie, its eyes are dark. Again you must remember that the light-colored birds don't necessarily follow these rules. Now, approximately at the time of the first molt, those dark eyes will change. The irises will develop a white or pearly color; this is another clue to the age of younger birds.

How does one know if a bird is one year old or fifteen

years old? Look at its feet. Small scales and small joints go with younger birds. Knobby joints and large scales suggest older birds. Also, look at the closed band. Read the date—just don't buy an unbanded bird.

If a sitting hen is attacked in her nest by another bird, you can be ninety-nine per cent sure that the invader is a female. These fights are frequently violent. Eggs are broken, and chicks are killed or thrown out. The adult birds may be lacerated, feathers may be pulled, and sometimes toes are chopped off. A hen budgie considers her nest box to be her castle. That small, curved, sharp, powerful beak is her one sure defense.

When Birds Don't Nest

Are you sure you have a pair? Really sure? Two friendly females might share a box, but a dozen infertile eggs is no great reward for all that effort.

The color of the cere is an excellent guide to recognizing sex, but only when the birds are in top breeding condition. At other times its color can be downright confusing.

Did you pattern your nest box after the standard design available in most pet shops? Granted, wild budgies find nest sites that were not made from rectangular pieces of plywood or hardboard, but remember that these birds can fly for miles, if need be, to find something that suits them. In a cage there is only your choice. I suggest that you purchase your first nest boxes and concaves from a pet shop.

Does the opening in the nest box face the light or dark? You might find that a rejected nest box will be accepted if you turn it to face a darker exposure.

Are there too many birds in the cage or aviary? Do they fight for the nest boxes? You should provide more boxes than you have hens so every pair can have a choice.

Does the nest box hang inside or outside the cage? Sometimes even this makes a difference, really. Hens that reject a nest box which hangs outside have been known to settle happily when the same box is hung inside the cage or aviary. They seem to like to creep over the outside before they go in.

Is the nest box similar to the one the bird was hatched

Eggs will hatch according to the order in which they were laid (*above*). Soft whitish down gives way to pin feathers, which are first noticeable on the wings (*below*) and then on the head and tail (*facing page*). Of the four nestmates, those that hatched first are farther along in development.

in? You may find that your bird is happier sitting in a box which resembles its birthplace.

Females fight harder, bite harder, and compete more strenuously for preferred nest boxes. Often during a fight between hens, eggs and chicks will be thrown out, and sometimes even the adults will be severely injured or killed. No kidding. What you should do, as I mentioned before, is to provide extra nest boxes and also remember not to crowd your breeding birds.

When Eggs Don't Hatch

It is natural for eggs to hatch; if they don't, it is important for you to know why. Should every egg hatch? Well, that would be nice, but it's highly unlikely. No breeder will get 100% of the eggs to hatch over the long haul. Should you have a number that rings a bell? Yes—I suggest that if your birds produce 90 fledglings from 100 eggs, you are doing your part adequately. A loss of only 10% (if you establish it is from a variety of causes) is something you and your birds can live with. On the other hand, if all your losses can be tied to just one symptom—such as all thin shelled, or all infertile, or all punctured shell, or all dead-in-shell—then you should try to search out the cause and correct it. Let's review some of the reasons why eggs don't hatch. Let's take them one at a time.

Broken eggs could be caused by thin shells—a dietary problem usually. I won't keep writing "usually"; in nature there is always the possibility of a second or third cause—that's only natural. If the hen hasn't been able to get enough lime from cuttlebone or oyster shell or mineral grit or chicken egg shell and enough vitamin D from food or food supplements or direct sunlight, then the egg shell suffers. Another possibility is that there is some poison present. Certain insecticides cause thin shells; DDT almost wiped out some Osprey colonies in the 1950s. However, dietary deficiency is the most likely cause of thin egg shells, which break.

Another cause of broken eggs is fighting in the nest box. Are your birds crowded? Is there another female in the cage or aviary who wants that nest box? The extra bird might make an excellent breeder if she had a proper mate and an equally desirable box elsewhere.

A punctured egg should warn you to check the length of the claws on your birds, especially the hens. If they are misshapen or especially long, trim them.

Infertile (clear) eggs under incubating hens suggest a "pair" of hens or an infertile male or incomplete copulation. Sometimes a young pair learns slowly; be patient, since there is nothing you can do or say to teach them. Sometimes in a crowded colony situation a pair are disturbed while they are copulating. Sometimes the female starts to sit in her nest box before she has been adequately inseminated. Sometimes the perch is too thin or too slippery for the hen to hold onto properly while the male is mating with her. Some fanciers go so far as to use square rather than round perches. Sometimes the male is permanently infertile because of disease or injury, or the male is temporarily infertile because of stress or poor diet. Sometimes coarse feathers around their vents keep the birds apart. Some fanciers check this and pluck some of the feathers if necessary.

Look at the cere. A female in breeding condition has a dark brown cere, and a male sports a bright, rich blue cere. The cere color in the albino and some dilute color varieties is washed out and will not help you—but then, you shouldn't be breeding albinos or other light colors if you are a beginner.

"Addled" eggs were fertilized but died during the incubation period. I will lump them with dead-in-shell. Dead-in-shell is discouraging because the birds got so close to success when something went wrong. If your aviary is cool and the female got off the clutch for over an hour, it is possible that all the embryos died in their shells from exposure to cold. Did you scare her off while inspecting the nest? Is there a cat in the bird room? Do rodents bother the birds at night? Do small children bother the birds day or night?

Another cause for dead-in-shell is that the chick could not cut its way out. Is there sufficient moisture? This is hard to measure, but if the problem is ever-present, you might try misting the clutch with 95 F. water from a fine spray. Don't soak the eggs, just a light, fine mist once a

Most budgie varieties can be grouped as blues or greens.

day. Also offer bath water and wet grass or wet leaves for the birds to roll in. The hen might just be smart enough to avail herself of what is needed. Moisture is a controversial issue; I'll have more to say about it later.

Still another common cause for dead-in-shell is a misshapen nest cavity. An egg may roll into a corner of the nest box and remain there, overlooked in the dark by the brooding hen bird. The remedy is under your control. Look at the bottom of the nest box. Is it possible for an egg to lodge in a corner? Well-designed commercial nest boxes are furnished with a removable wooden floor which has been hollowed on one side. Call it a concave—everyone else does—and be sure it was made to fit precisely in the nest box.

Addling may be caused by handling the eggs too much while the embryos are developing. The hen will turn her eggs with no help from you. Leave this job to her.

Remember that breeding birds is not like collecting stamps; you cannot do it by the numbers. But with constant vigilance and a minimum amount of thoughtful manipulation you can be a successful breeder not only of budgies but also of the "difficult" species.

Dirt on egg shells is liable to plug up some of the porous surface through which respiration takes place. The embryo can suffocate if the egg shell is especially dirty. If necessary, you can change the concave and even add a little punky wood or wood chips.

There is a long and windy story that ends up with this punch line: "Zana's Law states that if you fool with something long enough, it's bound to break." That's the "law"; now let's see how it can be applied to the breeding of budgies. A breeder of budgies segregates the sexes until he decides the "season" is about to begin. Then, after careful study of each adult bird available, pairs are chosen and placed in breeding cages where the hens immediately go to nest and proceed to lay and incubate infertile eggs. A month later it is obvious that all that occurred was a waste of effort and a loss of time. The breeder kept the sexes apart so they would not wear themselves out reproducing themselves. Then the breeder did some matchmaking. Then the breeder decided that the breeding season should start. Then the breeder popped the pairs he chose into cages furnished with nest boxes, and the hens popped into those nest boxes so eagerly that they forgot to give their mates an opportunity to make a contribution to the reproductive process. Result: five or more infertile eggs per nest box, laid on alternate days, which works out to ten days or more, and then an additional eighteen days of fruitless incubation—unless the bird breeder candles the eggs and interrupts the process.

When a hen is ready to lay, you cannot stop her by not furnishing a nest box. She will lay on a perch. When a hen is ready to incubate, you cannot stop her by stealing her eggs. She will incubate a golf ball. If eggs are infertile, first assume that *you* are the culprit. Many infertile eggs are the result of the application of Zana's Law.

So, to summarize: give your birds an opportunity to breed without manipulation. If the eggs are infertile, then look to an incompetent cock, or an impotent cock, or the remote but ever present possibility that you are looking at a pair of hens. I suggest that a beginner will lose less by keeping pairs together in an enclosure with extra nest boxes than by getting into a complicated management procedure. There is a lot to learn. Breed some birds this simple way first. There will be plenty of time later to fool around with controlled breeding.

When Nestlings Die

Don't be hasty to diagnose what went wrong when nestlings die; there are many possibilities and sometimes there are several concurrent causes. Ideally, a nest will contain four to six eggs. As they hatch, the older chicks begin to generate heat which tends to help incubate the still unhatched eggs. This is the ideal situation. Now let's consider some of the things that might go wrong.

Crushed nestlings are sometimes that way because they barely had the strength to cut their way out of their egg shells. Hatching exhausted them.

A cold nest box induces hens to sit tight, maybe too tight. The ever-loving hen on a singleton does not represent the ideal situation. A single chick from a clutch of just one egg does not enjoy the cushioning protection of

The youngsters in this clutch of five range in age from three to eleven days. Photo: Michael Gilroy.

eggs and other chicks. All the weight of the hen presses on the one baby bird. You might add a few dummy eggs to the concave until the chick gains strength. A concave with no dry, powdered feces, no punky wood, no wood chips provides no protection.

Often a deformed or diseased chick is crushed because it cannot compete with its siblings for food. If its cries are weak and it is ignored at mealtime, but seems to have a well-formed body, you might be able to save it by giving it a few supplemental feedings. If it is stunted or obviously deformed, you should put it down promptly.

Single chicks don't always cry loudly enough for food to keep parent birds going with enthusiasm. If you have two nests going at about the same age, take that single and put it in the other nest. Budgies cannot count.

Once in a while you may find a chick whose crop is inflated with air, really puffed—not full of regurgitated food, but full of air. This could kill the chick if it is not corrected. Sterilize a needle and pierce the balloon. You may have to repeat the process daily for as long as a week before the condition is alleviated. That tiny needle hole will close up quickly and heal in only a few hours.

A single chick in a concave sometimes becomes spread-eagled. Its legs are bent away from its body, and they become so stiff in that position that they cannot be drawn up normally. By then it is too late to help, but if you catch it in time, treat it like a crushed chick and simply put one or two infertile eggs or dummy eggs in the concave to relieve the pressure of the tightly brooding hen.

The hen should feed each newly hatched chick within four to six hours after hatching. If she doesn't, something is wrong, but all is not lost. Get some Pablum and glucose into the little chick, and it may then perk up enough to demand and get parental feeding. Don't look for opportunities to take over with hand-rearing, but if necessary, resort to it, preferably on a temporary basis.

Budgie parents will kill deformed or diseased chicks, and the others in the clutch will thrive and prosper. Males that want to breed again can be frustrated because the chicks are still in the nest or are in and out of the nest constantly; sometimes under these conditions a cock will attack his own chicks and may maul them severely. If you see or sense this coming on, there are several things you can do. These are all manipulations of the last resort—ideally, you need do nothing.

You could separate the chicks from their parents. Now you need another cage or a partition in the aviary. You must be sure the chicks can feed themselves. Offer them plenty of soft, soaked food, sprouted seed, hard-boiled egg (diced), and milksop. Put them in an enclosure with an older bird who might feed them or at least teach them how to hull seed.

You could separate the chicks and the cock from the hen in her nest box. If she has been thoroughly inseminated, she might start a new clutch of fertile eggs, and the cock will have a few days to wean the chicks. Then he can be put back with his mate. Give the chicks a new nest box that smells like the old one.

You could put an additional nest box in the enclosure with the pair and their chicks. The adults probably will move into the new box and leave the chicks with their old birthplace. The chicks will still get some food from the cock, and they will also get wise very quickly. I prefer this technique since it requires less from the bird keeper.

Young budgies will return to their nest box constantly. They will look around at the wide, wide world and then pop back into their place of security, especially if they are frightened, tired, or cold. This is perfectly normal behavior. They crave the security of that old nest box; don't deprive them of it without sufficient cause.

Just as an ideal breeding arrangement requires the infectious stimulation of three or more pairs close to each other, so an ideal nest contains more than just one chick. The parent birds are more likely to be encouraged or induced to feed by the clamor of three or four chicks than by the feeble squeaks of just a singleton. Possibly the chicks squeak even louder if they are competing for parental attention.

If a singleton nestling is not getting its crop stuffed fully by its parents and another nest with similar-sized birds is available, it might be a wise thing to put that

This bird has been afflicted with french molt, a disease that affects feather growth. Loss of feathers results in bare patches and gives the bird an unsightly look.

In contrast with the bird on the facing page, the feathers have developed normally on these birds.

single one into the other nest even if it has not been thoroughly rejected. Make sure the waif ends up smelling like its new nestmates and not like your fingertips or like his old nest box. When transferring the chick, use a plastic spoon, or wear rubber gloves, or, at the very least, don't hold the bird in your palm. A little dust from the new concave rubbed on the fostered bird will also make its acceptance even more certain.

A beginning budgie breeder should not look for opportunities to manipulate his birds or their eggs. This switch is one of the few I would endorse, and then only under special conditions of distress. The only other compelling reason a beginner has for handling nestlings is to band them.

Pigeon keepers have accumulated and recorded their experiences for perhaps two thousand years, and one interesting observation that has stood the test of time for them (and I believe for budgies too) is that powdered, dry droppings in a nest are beneficial. Nests wet with droppings are to be avoided at all costs, but dry feces will absorb the moisture from subsequent excretions, and the nestlings will remain clean and dry on a bed of dry waste. Also, the odor that the birds become accustomed to is critical. So, don't clean a nest completely, and don't swap eggs or chicks without dusting them with some of this material. This may make the difference between rejection or acceptance of a fostered squeaker.

Misting, Spraying, and Dipping

In a previous section we considered the possibility that dead-in-shell might come about as a result of lack of moisture. Some recognized experts advise us to mist, spray, or even dip budgie eggs in order to ensure sufficient moisture for improving hatchability. Other experts advise the reader not to do these things. I never found it necessary to mist or spray or dip, but it is unfair and unscientific to apply my experience universally.

Do you live in arid Albuquerque or in tepid Tallahassee? Is your bird room air-conditioned or electrically heated? Do your birds have an opportunity to bathe, roll in wet grass, sit in a screened-top aviary, and get rained on? This is a problem for you and your birds to work out, but I do suggest again that in the beginning you would do better to avoid manipulation. The dangers from adding moisture outweigh the risk of omitting this procedure, at least until you have had the personal experience of raising at least a hundred birds *in your own establishment.*

When Feathers Break

This is an unfair slap at the French, who, for all we know, are absolutely innocent of any wrongdoing or contribution to this bothersome disease. While it is commonly called french molt, the origin is unknown and the cure is unknown, but the diagnosis is easy. The feather shaft of a fledgling seems to decompose at its origin in the flesh and it breaks. Usually the primary and secondary wing feathers and the long tail feathers are the only ones involved, but sometimes even the body feathers are stricken.

Birds are affected at about the time they leave the nest. If you see this feather-shaft failure, pluck those feathers immediately; if the disease doesn't involve too many feathers, the bird may recover completely and develop normally thereafter. Some birds are so badly affected that they never develop normal feathering, and if they are permitted to live, they are incapable of flight and are known as "runners."

There is a tremendous amount of literature and speculation and research on this subject, but suffice it to say that at the time of this writing there is no incontrovertible evidence as to the cause of the nagging and unpredictable malady. Red mites and poor nutrition have been the targets of much study, but there is no proof.

Bar-Heads

In most budgie varieties there can be a pattern of transverse dark bars starting right about the cere and running up over the head. This pattern is proof positive that the bird has not had its first molt yet. This is the period when a youngster is most vulnerable to disease.

It is important to regularly check the nest boxes (*above*) to see that chicks have hatched without difficulty (*below*) and that the parents are feeding them.

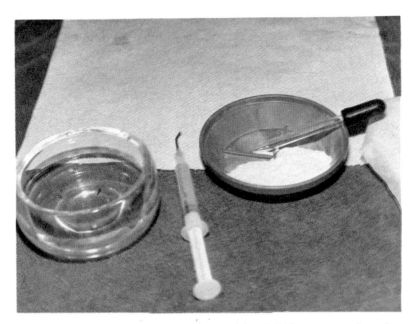

When parent birds fail to care for and feed their young, a breeder must step in and hand-rear the chicks to ensure their survival. An eyedropper and a syringe with feeding tube (*above*) can be useful in hand-rearing, especially if the chick is still small (*below*).

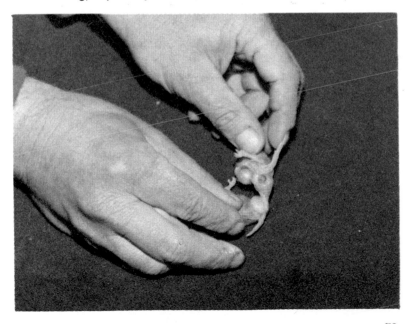

Some learn to hull their seeds and some don't. Some get enough to eat, but others are intimidated—these hang back and go light, catch cold or some digestive ailment, and soon you have a sick bird or a cageful of sick birds. That first molt and the loss of the barred head markings takes place at about three months of age.

Many experienced breeders of high-quality budgies will segregate the sexes until they are a year old. Now and then a bar-head will go to nest and raise a clutch; but this doesn't mean it's right. Until the first molt is completed, and especially during those first few days after the youngsters leave the nest, there are several things you can do to help them get started. Keep an old cock in with young birds; he might actually feed a few until they are more completely weaned. He might by example teach them to hull seed. Offer more millet. Millet is easier to hull than canary seed, and that should help as the youngster learns to feed itself. Offer supplemental sprouted seed, soaked seed, hulled millet, fresh scalded milk soaked up into stale bread or toast (called milksop), and diced hard-boiled eggs. None of these foods will teach a budgie to hull a canary seed, but they will surely keep it alive until it does learn.

Don't rush the youngsters out of the breeding cage. The cock might well continue to help them while the hen is starting her next clutch. This is where extra nest boxes could save the day.

Hand-Rearing

This is not a suitable subject for a book about breeding budgies simply. It is certainly not simple and it is usually not necessary. A waif might be fostered by budgies more effectively than you can do it. If you have three pairs tending to their young simultaneously, there is a good chance that one of these pairs can foster one or two abandoned or kicked-out youngsters. If all else fails, you might have a go at it. Remember that a pair of budgies will be kept busy constantly in order to raise their babies. Small meals fed frequently are the rule. Can you afford the time? Do you have the dexterity?

If you succeed, you will find that a hand-reared budgie is usually very tame, more like a feathered human than a captive bird. Most hand-reared birds do not make good parents in a breeding establishment. So, for breeding stock, avoid these hand-raised pets. As pets they are the most amusing and charming birds you could possibly imagine—so make up your mind and act accordingly. Just remember that you cannot have it both ways.

If you must start with a day-old chick, you will need a brooder or its equivalent. These devices are used for quail, poultry, and ducks all the time. They are expensive, but they do work. A hen will brood her chick until it is about a week old almost as intensively as she incubated her eggs. The newly hatched chick gets its body heat from its mother and its older siblings by conduction. After about a week of brooding, the bird is less reptilian. It becomes "warm-blooded," and it maintains its body temperature by oxidizing food for the remainder of its life. So, during that first week you must pump in heat at about 95 F. to keep that little machine going.

Feed the chick off a broomstraw or with a syringe which you can buy from various pet dealers or bird breeders' supply companies. The moisture the chick needs must accompany the food it gets, so make sure that you don't neglect moistening what you offer. Start with sweetened baby cereal and add hulled, crushed, soaked millet. Health-food stores frequently carry a high-quality hulled millet.

Keep the crop as full as the bird will have it. When it begs, feed it until it ceases to beg. Start to feed a chick by putting it on its back. It will open its mouth and squeak. Touch its mouth with some slightly sweetened, damp Pablum or crushed, hulled, soaked millet on a broomstraw and go on from there. The preferred sweetener is glucose, but honey or sugar will also work. In a few weeks you will be exhausted, and the chick will be growing feathers.

Congratulations. Now try to wean the chick. Remember that this was your idea in the first place. Most chicks will rapidly learn to hull seed by being in the company of other birds, but a lone chick will likely survive, regardless.

Large-scale budgie breeders often find it economical to prepare their own seed mixtures in bulk (*above*), and some add pellets to this mixture (*below*). Feed hoppers (*facing page*) provide a constant supply of seed for a large number of birds.

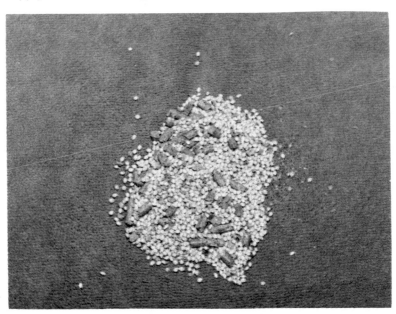

When Breeders Die

Accidents can happen to any of us, or to any of our birds. We try to anticipate hazards and reduce risks. Cages must be tight. Doors must latch securely. Nest boxes must be fastened so as not to fall off their shelves or hooks. Simple intelligence dictates these precautions. Now consider a few you may not have thought of.

Budgies tend to be quiet at night. If a door is slammed or a light flashes, all the birds will be upset. Some will fly into obstructions, and others will desert their nests, especially if the light goes out completely before they can find their way back. Chilled eggs, fractured skulls, broken necks, and heart attacks can follow night-time disturbances. Dogs, cats, rodents, and even human visitors, especially at night, can cause chaos. This is something you must control.

A really dedicated cock may starve to death while he is busy feeding his mate as she broods her eggs and nestlings. Look at his crop. If it is **always** empty, you and he have a problem. He will be malnourished, weak, cold, and may even move into the nest box to keep warm. This is his undoing, since all he can get there is hungrier. If necessary, you should isolate such a cock long enough to get him to feed himself. The female will then get out of her nest box long enough to get food for herself and her chicks. With luck, conditions will improve.

Mites can weaken a nesting bird and be the "straw that broke the camel's back." Mite control is not too difficult; dusts and sprays from your pet dealer will be very useful. Read the directions and follow them carefully.

Sudden, unexplained deaths take place among all creatures at all times. Be reconciled. You will never know the real reason for every one, but if you lose only one or two birds out of a score in the course of a year, from causes you cannot explain, you can figure that this is the normal mortality of any population. Heart attacks, apoplexy, and broken necks from flying into obstructions are bound to happen.

Nutrition

Here we consider food and water and food supplements—except grit, which is discussed separately.

In Australia, Forshaw (in *Parrots of the World*) tells us, budgies "feed on seeds procured on or near the ground." When we look at a map of the range of budgies, we find that they are everywhere except along most of the coastline and the northern tropical woodlands. Today aviculturists consider the caged budgie as a domesticated bird, nearly as domesticated as the barnyard goose, duck, or pigeon; certainly as domesticated as the canary, which has been cage-bred for perhaps as many as four hundred years. So we can forget the names of the Australian wild grasses which wild budgies eat.

Today, captive, domesticated budgies eat only what we feed them, and they thrive. They are surely bigger and (I believe) better looking than their wild ancestors. If you have perhaps three pairs of breeders with their young, you should be buying your seed in bulk rather than in the convenient cartons of mix available in bird stores and pet shops. The packaged mix is excellent, make no mistake about that. The companies that put it up are respected worldwide for their competence and integrity. The only drawback is that the cost of packaging makes the food expensive if you are feeding more than one or two birds.

A good mix will contain approximately one part canary seed and one part millet. To this, many breeders add 10% clipped or hulled oats. Some advocate soaking the oats in water for twenty-four hours before offering this high-protein food. A clipped oat is an ordinary oat seed which has had the rough end of its hull chopped off—horses love them. Hulled oats have had all the hull removed—horses love them too. I might mention here that canary seed (*Phalaris canariensis*) is the name of a particular plant seed; it is not a mixture of various plant seeds developed to feed canaries. If canary seed is available in various sizes, you should opt for just a little of the smaller size. The greater proportion of the canary seed should be the larger-sized seeds. Millets (*Panicum*

Greenfood is an important part of the budgerigar diet. Rye grass (*above*) can be grown at home, and seed can be germinated too (*below*); the grass and sprouts can then be offered to the birds.

Some breeders find that their birds enjoy grated carrot (*above*) and spinach (*below*). Carrot is best placed in a tray set up at the feeding station, while leafy spinach leaves should be fastened to the flight wires.

and *Setaria*) also come in several sizes, varieties, and colors. Colors are meaningless. I suggest you offer a blend of the larger sizes. Thus you hedge your bets in case one farm field was better provided with the minerals which the birds also derive from their food. You need not offer your birds sunflower seed. Most budgies do not eat them, but since they are high in fat, a bird in need of special care might well be offered some.

Today most successful budgie breeders agree that fresh, leafy vegetables and fresh fruits like grape and apple are important elements of the diet and not simply treats for now and then. Your job is to provide a constant supply and to remove what remains uneaten before it wilts. Lettuce, spinach, kale, broccoli, and ordinary garden rye grass are all fine greens. Just be sure they are not covered with any insecticidal spray.

When the birds are raising their chicks, you might also offer a little milksop—scalded milk on dry bread or toast is great, and a little can also be fed to bar-heads as they learn to feed themselves.

Remember that budgies hull the seed they eat, and usually the hulls fall back into the feeding dish. Be careful to make sure that the chaff is not mistaken for seed. You can blow the chaff away, or buy a gadget to separate the seed from the chaff. This is your problem and you must solve it. You will find references to this problem even in the Holy Bible.

Food supplements, liquid vitamins, and the like are all insurance against problems caused by poor nutrition, but I believe that if you provide the basic seeds, green food, fruit, milksop, and clean, fresh water, then these "insurance" items become just that, rather than necessities.

Oh yes, cuttlebone or oyster shell is necessary as a supplemental source of lime unless you feed your birds 20-minute hard-boiled egg *with the shell included*. Boil the egg thoroughly, since some viral diseases of poultry may be transmitted through the egg; we know that twenty minutes at 212 F. will eliminate the hazard. I provide cuttlebone *and* the egg shell. The diced hard-boiled egg is especially valuable when there are chicks to be fed.

You should test your millet and canary seed to be sure it is alive. Live seed is known to provide nutritional benefits not obtainable from dead seed. Permit a sample of seed to germinate on a piece of wet towel for a few days. Most of it should sprout. Don't waste it—the birds will eat it. If you can afford the time, you are well advised to feed any budgie some sprouted seed routinely; but remember that the basis of the budgie diet is dry millet and canary seed.

In pigeon literature there is a good deal about pigeon "milk," a substance generated by the breeding birds as their eggs hatch. It is described as being easy to digest, full of nutrients, and with precisely the right amount of moisture. "A unique marvel of nature" is the way it is presented to the reader. Well, it is surely a marvel of nature—but it is not unique. Parrots do something similar. A day-old budgie hatchling is fed a moist mash which certainly contains substances modified by storage in the parents' crop. Let's say crops since much of the food consumed by a hatchling budgie in its first week was eaten initially by the cock; then he regurgitated it and fed it to the hen, who finally passed it on to the chick. This food goes into a nest with a half-dozen chicks spanning nearly two weeks of age. We observe that the youngest birds get the finest, softest part of this food. All those birds jammed into that same dark nest—now that is something to marvel at!

Normal, healthy budgies will spend a good part of their time demolishing the wooden parts of the nest box, the cage, and the very perches they sit on. Their muscles are powerful and their mandibles are sharp. I don't know why they do it, but make no mistake, they surely will.

Your first responsibility is to ensure that there is nothing poisonous that they can gain access to. Wood should not be treated with creosote or other preservatives, fungicides, insecticides, or paints containing heavy metals such as lead, or known poisons such as phosphorous, selenium, or arsenic. If in doubt, keep it out.

Next, I suggest you offer substitutes for the furniture which will satisfy their desire to chew. Try twigs of just about any fruit tree except cherry. Just be sure it was

In addition to the basic seed diet (*above*), provide your budgerigars with cuttlebone and mineral blocks (*below*). Grit can be offered in a hopper (*facing page*) or in a dish, whichever is more convenient.

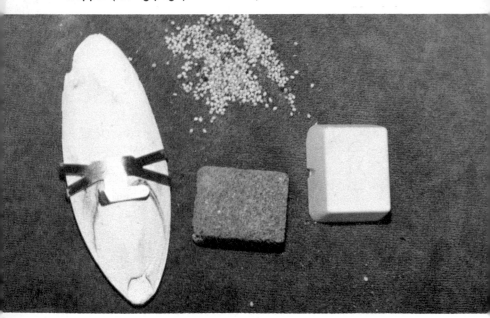

not sprayed for at least several months prior. Thin twigs of all but the evergreens (resinous) and laurels (poisonous) and perhaps the cherry (also possibly poisonous) are avidly worked over by budgies. Willow—both the tree and the pussy willow bush—are great. Also try maple, birch, mulberry, beech, and forsythia. Oak, walnut, and other nut trees tend to be high in tannic acid; although this is not a potent poison, it is probably less desirable for our purpose. Your birds will enjoy crawling over and picking over bundles of freshly cut twigs.

Perches of bark-covered branches and twigs will work out well in any cage or aviary. When they get dirty or worn or infested with mites, you can easily replace them. Some of the inner bark and soft leaf-buds you offer may be eaten. Most will be torn up and dropped. None will be used in nest making; this is the natural behavior for budgies in the wild and in the cage.

Grit

Everyone knows (because the books tell us) that the seed is hulled, swallowed, and stored in the crop, from which it descends to the gizzard, a tremendously powerful muscular organ containing bits of sand and tiny pebbles. Here, we learn, the grinding of the grain by the stone takes place, and then the porridge of crushed grain is passed into the intestine for digestion. Well, now we have ample evidence from a well-known and highly regarded veterinary surgeon that caged, seedeating birds do well or better if they never get any grit into their gizzards. So you pay your money and you take your choice.

Disease

I was forty or fifty years old before I really looked at this word, *disease*. Two syllables: *dis* = a want of, a lack of, the opposite of, and *-ease* = freedom from labor or pain or anxiety. There it is: "a lack of freedom from labor, pain, or anxiety."

Now, let's look at breeding or nonbreeding budgies and see what we can do to free them from labor, pain, or anxiety. First, consider a picture of health: The bird is plump but not fat. Its feathers are sleek, tight to its body. Few or no feathers are missing; none are broken or twisted. The body is smooth. There are no lumps, boils, cysts, lesions, or bare spots where feathers were removed and didn't grow back. The eyes are bright and not tearing. The other openings are also dry: nostrils, ears, mandibles, and vent are all free from moisture or matter. The scales on the feet and legs should be small and regular; there should be no unusual knobs or lumps. The claws—four on each foot (count them before you pay your money)—should be slightly curved but not corkscrewed and certainly not missing; a poor grip on the perch might lead to an unconsummated courtship and infertile eggs.

Choose birds that look like the ideal or as much like the ideal as you can afford. Don't put your first money on expensive color varieties, but rather invest it in close-banded, year-old birds of good form and excellent health.

Now, how are you to keep them that way? Plan to spend your initial efforts in preventing disease rather than on curing it. Practice simple hygiene. Most of it is just good sense, applied. Here is a quick checklist of things you should do to prevent disease. Most will cost you nothing; several will cost you dearly if you omit them.

Don't crowd your birds. The first pair in a large aviary or flight cage or alone in a breeding cage should have five cubic feet; for each additional pair two additional cubic feet is a minimum. A breeding cage for one pair should be at least 36 in. long and 18 in. high and wide. Then, when all five or so chicks are fledged, they can remain with their parents for an extra week or two without turmoil.

Arrange perches and receptacles so feces don't fall into the water or food. This only recycles disease germs and parasites, something you and your birds surely don't need. Bone-dry droppings in a nest concave are another matter; don't worry about them.

Quarantine any new bird for a month—some say six weeks—before you introduce it to your established breeding colony. This means that you should keep it in another room, not just in a separate cage. Be aware of

As perches, the advantages that tree branches (*above*) have over wooden dowels (*facing page*) is that they vary in thickness, thereby providing exercise for the birds, and they offer opportunities for gnawing as the birds chew off the bark.

the nature of bird-disease transmission and avoid it. Wash your hands; wear a freshly laundered smock; don't invite sneezing strangers into your bird room.

Use a No-Pest strip *occasionally*. Familiarity with these things breeds contempt for them. Soon the lice and ticks and mites will adapt themselves to the poison, and only you and your birds will suffer.

How can you be sure your bird room is not infested with insect or arachnid parasites? One indicator for the presence of those that bite or suck is your own skin or the skin of some "thin-skinned" person. If you sense or hear complaints of itching or stinging or tickling on anyone's exposed skin after you and/or they have visited the bird room, you can assume that at least one of many species of parasites is present. Don't assume that you can always see them. Many are truly microscopic, and these cannot be seen by the unaided human eye. In their mildest form, they are irritating pests. At their worst, they will debilitate your birds and may even transmit disease. Pet shops and aviary supply companies offer many pest-control substances which are safe for your birds. Should you use them?—yes. Should you spread them indiscriminately?—no. Is there one universal panacea?—no. **WARNING**: *When applying any pesticide on the birds or in the bird room, read the instructions and abide by them strictly.*

I will try to avoid the chicken-and-the-egg controversy in this short excursion, but you may think of it by yourself. If you look over a bunch of birds in a dealer's cage or in an aviary, you may see a skinny, bedraggled individual with a dirty vent, crusty feet, and a spongy cere. Examine it closely if you dare, and surely you will find it to be covered with parasites. There will be lice and mites and perhaps even a tick or two. Now look at the other birds. They will be plump and sleek and free of infestation. I don't know which came first, but I do know that parasites are more likely to be found on birds that are losing ground. Maybe this is "Nature's way" of clearing the decks.

Healthy, robust birds probably preen and are preened more. Perhaps there is a smell of death that attracts the parasites, or a smell of health that repels them. All this leads to my inescapable conclusion that a novice breeder has no business starting with anything less than fully flighted bar-heads or young mature birds in perfect physical condition.

It is possible that the hen will pluck a few breast feathers while she is in the nest box in order to enlarge the warm bare-skin area available for incubating eggs. You may find such feathers on the concave; but somehow they never look like they were placed there, rather they were plucked and there is where they fell. There is, however, another kind of plucking which is intolerable: here a parent bird plucks the young. Sometimes it is caused by environmental conditions which bring on stress. Flashing lights, banging on cages, noises, smoke, vermin, a hovering cat, cooking odors, crowding, lack of a second nest box—the list is endless but logical if you are willing to patiently think about it. If you correct everything that seems wrong but still cannot stop a particular bird from plucking the chicks, get that offender out of your bird room. Such a bird doesn't belong in a breeding establishment; it might nevertheless make a good single pet.

Give your birds twelve hours of uninterrupted rest per day, in draft-free quarters with only a dim night-light to permit safe return to the nest or perch if they are disturbed.

Be sure that feed and water containers are always full and clean.

Keep bird seed cool, dry, and vermin-free. Plastic tubs or metal cans are better than burlap or paper bags for storage of seed.

Control the temperature; avoid prolonged exposure of birds to less than 50 F. or more than 80 F.

Don't make change for change's sake. Plan ahead with cage furniture, perches, nest boxes, etc., and then try to leave things alone.

Get some spare nest-box concaves so you can insert a clean, dry, vermin-free concave if things get sticky or mite infested.

Cull sick and weak birds from the colony. Be ruthless. Sentiment has no place in a bird-breeder's room.

The title of this section is "Disease," but I've sug-

Budgies can be set up for breeding in colonies (*above and below*); in this way, they are given ample room for flight. In colony breeding, sometimes it is useful to fasten a holding cage (*facing page*) to the outside of the flight for the purpose of isolating individual birds or pairs.

gested no cures. That is precisely my point. Budgies are long lived, hardy, and disease resistant. Given good food and good accommodations and a wholesome, uncrowded environment, they will live ten or even twenty years and will be good producers for at least five years.

A hospital cage with thermostatically controlled temperature is a form of insurance. If you have several hundred birds, including some rare varieties, you might want to invest in such a cage. If you want one, don't build it; buy it. Buy a good one; choose a recognized brand; don't skimp.

A shelf of drugs is no way to start a campaign for breeding budgies without tears. I suggest you would be better prepared to cope with disease emergencies by owning a good book on the subject—see the section entitled "More About Budgies"—and by getting to know some other breeders. Join a specialty club. Pay dues. Go to meetings. Really, your birds will be healthier. You can count on your more experienced friends to help you in case things really get out of hand. Remember, you are getting into a hobby, not a cut-throat business.

I don't deny the value of medicines, but I do believe that many remedies are overworked substitutes for good nutrition and good environmental control.

Before you get into trouble, you should scout around for a veterinarian who is conversant with bird problems and is willing to take on something as small as a budgie. Remember that a veterinarian is a good professional doctor of medicine, and professional services are necessarily expensive. You must be prepared to pay for these services by the hour and not by the pound. This cost factor strengthens the justification for avoiding scrub birds for breeding stock. Junky birds are more prone to sicken, and if they do, it costs no less to care for them than it does for top-quality stock.

Psittacosis

This subject gets a separate heading because it will certainly be thrown at you by someone who is worried about human infection. Yes, it is remotely possible. No, it is not something that should deter anyone from keeping and breeding budgies.

Psittacosis is a pneumonia-type disease of birds which can be transmitted to people and which has proven fatal in the past at one time or another. The number of people who come down with psittacosis in the U.S.A. is far fewer than the number of people who are bitten by rattlesnakes. Today, with the wonder drugs, no one need die of this disease.

Don't assume that because a budgie sneezes, it has psittacosis, for birds are subject to many other respiratory diseases. Psittacosis gets a lot of attention from the uninformed because for many years the importation of psittacine birds was banned to eliminate the hazard of infection by this disease. Later it was established that although psittacine birds were sometimes involved, all birds could and do catch and transmit the disease. Properly, the disease should be called ornithosis (meaning a disease of all birds rather than just parrots). Duck pluckers and turkey-farm attendants have been infected, and so today's parrots are no longer considered the sole or very special culprits.

Today, prompt and complete cures of both birds and people can be effected by physicians using wonder drugs. Bear in mind that this disease, and many other diseases as well, is most likely to attack the weak, injured or malnourished.

What Is Dirty and What Is Not

Dead birds and ancient unhatched eggs and uneaten wilted greens and accumulated loose feathers and drinking water with feces in it—these are dirty; but dry gray droppings from healthy birds are not dirty. Pigeon keepers will tell you that their birds don't do well in new housing until there is a layer of bone-dry droppings on the floor! This, I believe, is true of budgies too.

Certainly dry droppings in the nest box are natural. Budgies themselves don't even try to remove anything until they are about to start another clutch. Then they might toss out some material if the nest box is too shallow as a result of the accumulation. Then again, they might not.

Dry droppings on the concave don't seem to support any bird pests, but they do form a cushion under the

This eleven-day-old youngster (*above*) sits in the concave that is commonly used in wooden nest boxes. Cock and hen (*facing page*) guard their nest with parental devotion. Photos: Michael Gilroy.

eggs and they do absorb moisture from fresh droppings and thereby keep the chicks clean. I would advise a beginner to be fastidiously careful to keep fruit, greens, water, and seed absolutely clean but not to invade the nest box during a breeding campaign unless there is a death or a disease which causes more wet droppings thàn the concave with its dry dust and sawdust can take care of. If the concave becomes convex, of course it should be scraped. You should not wash a concave and reinstall it immediately, as the wet wood in an active nest might cause the babies to sicken. Elsewhere I mentioned that spare concaves are a good insurance, and it bears repeating.

Companions

This is a book about how to breed budgies simply. So, keep it simple: no companions. That's simple.

If you have a large flight cage reserved for growing bar-heads, you might also warehouse a few Zebra Finches or Cockatiels with them, but in the breeding enclosure there should be just breeding pairs of budgies only. Those bar-heads might learn to bathe and perhaps even eat a wider variety of foods if they are housed with experienced older budgies or even other species of birds that do such things, but that is the only advantage to keeping bird companions in the budgie breeding room.

Budgies don't hybridize with other birds, nor do they share nest sites or otherwise socialize outside their species. So, I'll say it again: keep breeding budgies with other breeding budgies only. Also, as I mentioned elsewhere, this is desirable because budgies are known to stimulate each other to breed.

It is a fact that budgies cannot count. They cannot count the number of eggs in the nest, nor can they count the number of birds in a cage. Budgies can and do establish pecking orders on occasion, and if they do, the poor bird at the bottom of the ladder may have a rough life. One saving grace you might capitalize on, since they cannot count, is that if there are six or more similar-looking budgies in the same adequately sized enclosure, the low bird on the totem pole will frequently be ignored, forgotten, or lost in the ongoing process of living. With only two pairs, the birds can keep track of each other on an individual basis; but by the time there are a half-dozen adults and some babies on the way, the pecking order gets confused; it ceases to be clearly defined, and it is less of a burden on that bottom bird.

Birds in nearby cages can and do influence each other. If you want to break up a pair and remate them, you should get them completely out of sight and hearing of each other until new pair bonds are established.

Observations of the social life of large flocks of wild budgies provide convincing evidence that they stimulate each other to breed. Though conditions are right, an isolated pair may sit and bill and coo, but may never make a move into a nest box. That same pair in the company of two or more additional pairs will produce as many as twenty chicks a year! I don't recommend such intensive breeding, but it does happen that way.

Must they all be in the same enclosure? No, but it helps. How about stacked cages? Yes, this seems to be close enough to trigger the love bug.

Budgies are not "difficult" birds. Their requirement checklist is relatively short: simple nutrition, temperate warmth, a few spare nest boxes, and some more budgies nearby. Maybe because it is so easy, some of us get careless and try shortcuts. For those of us who follow the rules, budgies are so easy that not only can you manipulate their eggs and young, but you can even use this species to foster Cockatiels. Now, the Cockatiel is relatively shy and is usually considered to be a bird you move up to, rather than a beginner's bird. Well, if you should decide, after mastering budgies to a move up and you have fertile Cockatiel eggs from a hen that refuses to sit, just put one or two of those Cockatiel eggs under a sitting budgie, and she will carry them at least far enough so that you can hand-rear the nestlings the rest of the way. Remember that a cockatiel is twice the size of a budgie; it needs more room and much more food.

Banding and Recording

The budgie breeder who does not band all nestling birds with closed bands is missing the boat. The first few

Record keeping is especially important to breeders. An advantage prefabricated cardboard nest boxes *(above)* have over wooden ones *(facing page)* is that one can write directly on them. Banding *(below)* enables individual birds to be permanently identified. Facing-page photo: Penny Corbett and Stephanie Logue.

babies will be easy to remember, you think. Well, you think wrong on two counts. First, if you end up with twenty or so offspring after the first year, you cannot hope to remember each bird and its parentage. This is important if you spot a genetic defect or if you spot an unusually good youngster. The band will provide the clue to its parentage if you take the next step and keep a record of what happened.

Second, if you want to sell a bird, your customer will pay a premium for a closed band on the budgie. He wants to know how old it is, the color of its parents, and where he got it. You might want to know later on if that bird was paid for or stolen. So, band your birds when they are between six and ten days old. If the bird is too small, the band will fall off. If too large, you won't be able to slip one on. Watch carefully and remember that in a clutch of five there could be twelve days difference in age between the youngest and oldest bird.

If the adults didn't have permanent bands when you got them, you should install some plastic or metal numbered bands which can then be recorded to get the information on paper. I suggest a book or a file of 3 × 5 index cards. Every bird should get a card. It should show the number of that bird and the number of each of its parents. Also, you should enter its sex when it becomes obvious. Finally, leave a space to write in how the bird was disposed of: sale, put down, died, or whatever. On the back of the card you might write something about its color, conformation, or how well it does as a breeder.

You might file by date or by number—actually the number is better since it will be easier to find the card if you start looking with the bird in hand.

Join a budgerigar club and use their bands or purchase a set from advertisers in the avicultural magazines. The numbered metal bands are either dated and/or permanently colored so you can determine the age of the bird at a glance, even without referring to its file card. There is not much to be gained from an index of cards which refers to pairs. Budgies don't mate for life unless you ordain it, and for every breeding season you may arrange new matings.

When you are ready to band your first squeaker, you should work alone. Sit down on a comfortable chair in front of a steady table. Hold the baby bird in one hand with its feet pointing up. It will make a racket even if it isn't being hurt. You may put the band on either leg. Point three toes forward and slip the band over them; then slide it up the leg until it clears the claw of the fourth toe. You may need a round toothpick or a sharpened wooden matchstick to get that last toe through the band. Pigeon keepers sometimes use a bit of petroleum jelly to ease the job, and I've seen budgie banders apply a little saliva. It really isn't difficult after you have done it once. The timing is really the critical part of the project. It is highly unlikely that you will ever have two chicks from the clutch that are both ready to be banded at the same time. Remember, banding is but half the job. You must record the data promptly to make it meaningful.

If the squeaker is too small, the band may fall off, and if the hen doesn't like the band, she might remove it. The dexterity of a budgie is a source of constant surprise to everyone who has ever kept one. Band removal from an undersized juvenile is duck soup for a budgerigar. I'm waiting to read the mystery novel in which the murderer trained a budgie to open the door or insert the poison or light the fuse.

Breeder's Jargon

Here is a very short glossary of words a beginning breeder will hear or see as the hobby continues to take hold. You will encounter many words and expressions which are not used outside aviculture and are probably unnecessary even in aviculture, but now you are hooked and you cannot escape.

Ornithology. The study of birds. From the Greek *ornis,* "a hen, a bird"; and *-ology,* "the study of."

Aviculture. The care of birds. From the Latin *avis,* "bird"; and *cultus,* "care."

Psittacine. From the Greek *psittakos,* which means "parrot."

Parrot. A bird with a hooked bill and two of its four toes

83

Proper budgie maintenance includes checking the water bottles each day (*above*). Some breeders feel it is important to spray water into the flights (*below*). Since many budgies are not inclined to bathe, spraying helps keep their plumage in good condition (*facing page*).

pointing forward. From the French *perroquet,* a diminutive of *Pierre,* "Peter."

Parakeet. Parrots with long, tapering tails.

Budgerigar. The small parrot *Melopsittacus undulatus.* Probably from Australian Aboriginal *budgaree,* "something good, fine, handsome, pretty, or something good to eat."

Melopsittacus undulatus. The present scientific name of the budgerigar. *Melos* is from the Greek and means "song." *Psittacus,* as noted above, means "parrot." *Undulatus,* a Latin word, means "wavy" and refers to the wavy pattern on the wing feathers of the bird. Shaw was the first to describe the bird, although it seems to have been discovered by John Gould.

Bar-head. Juvenile before its first molt.

Inbreeding. Either parent is mated to the offspring; also, brother-sister or cousin matings; that is, close relatives are mated.

Line breeding. Matings not closer than cousins but still intended to retain established genetic features; that is, inbreeding of distantly related individuals.

More About Budgies

It is unnecessary to become a pioneer until after you reach a frontier. Applied to aviculture, budgies included, most of us never get far enough to press at the outer limits. We should consider ourselves fortunate if we are able to keep in the swim. Well, that's all right. It's still a lot of fun, it teaches us something, it challenges, it rewards. So I humbly suggest that, as you read this book and start out with your first breeders, you practice some humility. Assume that there are already plenty of tricks known to the trade. Learn what others already have mastered before you design a new nest box or feeder or cage or aviary or procedure.

First, subscribe to *American Cage-Bird Magazine;* write to them at 3448 North Western Avenue, Chicago, IL 60618. The magazine is published monthly, and it runs about sixty pages per issue. You will find not only articles about aviculture but advertisements for birds, food, books, and cages. Also, there is usually a section devoted to associations and shows. You will find that these societies and associations welcome new members and will provide help and support which cannot be found in any book.

Second, read more about budgies, from a number of authors. Even if they don't necessarily agree on all points, each will present an opinion based on experience which should be useful to you. Here, then, are some books I have read and found worthwhile.

* *Budgerigar Handbook* by Ernest H. Hart. Hart is an American budgie pioneer and a highly competent bird artist. This book is not out of print, although he wrote it back in 1961, which is certainly a tribute to its usefulness. I took some of the photographs so, understandably, I too think it's great!

* *Diseases of Budgerigars* by Cessa Feyerabend (1970) is precisely that. This is a 128-page hardcover book with clear drawings of bill defects, skeletal structure, anatomy, and the best illustrations I've seen for identifying the common lice and mites which afflict budgies. The language is not technical, but the important facts are presented in such a form that even a veterinarian could find them useful. It is not puffed with pictures of pretty birds or medicine bottles, but rather it is full of the information you will appreciate having at arm's reach. Now that I've seen it, I would not be without it.

Budgerigars in Color by A. Rutgers, edited by Cyril H. Rogers. This book was originally written in Dutch, but the Rogers version is in easy-to-read English. The color plates are all from paintings by the famous illustrators R. A. Vowles and H. Heinzel.

Best in Show by Gerald S. Binks was published in 1974 and is, far and away, the best, complete, up-to-date budgie book I've seen. The color photos are extremely sharp and were chosen to further clarify an already clear text. Binks covers all the aspects of budgie keeping that I can think of, and some I hadn't thought of. Read Binks!

Budgerigars by Cyril H. Rogers (1970) is strongest on color breeding. This is where it will prove most useful to an advanced bird keeper.

* *Budgerigars* by George A. Radtke is a well-

Many breeders, like John B. Hunter (*above*), a well-known Scottish bird fancier, like the challenge of competition at bird shows. Exhibition Budgerigars (*facing page*) are not placed in competition with ordinary budgies (*below*) at shows. Top photo: Michael Gilroy; facing-page photo: Harry V. Lacey.

illustrated 90-page primer. It was translated from a 1968 German text.

* *Parrots and Parrot-like Birds* is a classic but sometimes controversial book. It was written by a most interesting British aviculturist, the Most Noble Hastings William Sackville Russell, the Twelfth Duke of Bedford, Marquess of Tavistock, etc. Born in 1888, he died tragically of accidental gunshot in 1953 while hunting a hawk. This predator was threatening a flock of free-flying, homing budgies on his estate near Tavistock in Devonshire, England. Now the Duke accomplished things with parrots that were truly wonderful. He maintained and bred varieties in outdoor aviaries which others could hardly manage indoors, but some authorities today believe that he kept his tropical birds in an environment which was unduly harsh. Englishmen, it is suggested, may love Devonshire, but equatorial parrots might well do better with something sunnier and warmer. He also was a stickler for a spartan diet, so again there are some who believe the birds would have done better with a more generous supply of oily and high-protein foods. But small technical criticisms notwithstanding, this man was an avicultural giant, and his book is surely required reading for anyone who wants to know more about budgies and their ilk. Think of it—a flock of free-flying, homing budgies in Devonshire, England!

Encyclopedia of Cage and Aviary Birds by Cyril H. Rogers (1975) is a large-format, 200-page book with about thirty pages devoted to budgies, and several pages of good color plates in addition. The sections on color inheritance are clear and well organized. The chapters entitled "Housing" and "Breeding" are also especially valuable. C. H. Rogers is a competent British aviculturist. The book was edited by Dr. Val Clear, who is a popular American author of bird literature. The other cage birds covered in the book are the species which one is most likely to encounter. If you are interested in a broader base than budgies alone, this book should be most valuable.

* *Parrots of the World* by Joseph M. Forshaw, illustrated by William T. Cooper (1977) has gone through

several printings. My copy was published by T.F.H. Publications, and I refer to it repeatedly. The book consists of nearly 600 large pages and contains a full-color painting of every parrot species. There are also chapters on the classification, physical attributes, and natural history of these birds. When parrot keepers are in doubt, they should start with Forshaw and Cooper.

* *Building an Aviary* by Carl Naether and Matthew Vriends (1978) is the book to read *before* starting on any bird-housing construction projects.

* *Published by T.F.H. Publications*

"Stop the Train, I Want to Get Off!"

How do we induce budgies to breed? I think by now you know: several pairs, proximity of an adequate number of nest boxes and spares, good nutrition, etc., etc.

But now the axe has fallen. You have been told by parent or spouse to quit filling the place with birds. So naturally you tell the person that once budgies get going, it's *simply impossible* to stop them. However, if you must, you could remove their nest boxes and separate the sexes and keep the chicks in with a parent. Then perhaps things will slow down a bit. Good luck!

Both the owners of single hand-tamed budgies (*above*) and of breeding pairs (*facing page*) will find a bird carrier (*below*) handy whenever it becomes necessary to transport their birds.

Index

Budgerigar parents and nestlings. Photo: Harry V. Lacey.